FACING DIVORCE

BY STEPHANIE FINNE

BLUE OWL
BOOKS

TIPS FOR CAREGIVERS

Social and emotional learning (SEL) helps children manage emotions, create and achieve goals, maintain relationships, learn how to feel empathy, and make good decisions. The SEL approach will help children establish positive habits in communication, cooperation, and decision-making. By incorporating SEL in early reading, children will be better equipped to build confidence and foster positive peer networks.

BEFORE READING

Talk to the reader about divorce. Help explain what it is and how it will affect him or her.

Discuss: What is divorce? What changes will happen after divorce?

AFTER READING

Divorce happens to many families. Discuss this with the reader. Explain that it is not the child's fault. Remind him or her that he or she is not alone.

Discuss: What emotions do you feel? Does the reader have friends with divorced parents? What emotions did they feel?

SEL GOAL

Children dealing with divorce may struggle with anger and frustration. Help readers find healthy outlets for those feelings. Have students write down things that they do when they are angry that make them feel better. Help them come up with new ideas, such as nonaggressive physical activities or mindfulness exercises. Explain how these can help with anger and frustration.

TABLE OF CONTENTS

CHAPTER 1
What Is Divorce? 4

CHAPTER 2
What Does It Mean? 8

CHAPTER 3
What about Me? 16

GOALS AND TOOLS
Grow with Goals 22
Mindfulness Exercise 22
Glossary 23
To Learn More 23
Index 24

WHAT IS DIVORCE?

Noah's parents have been fighting all the time. One day, they want to talk to Noah. They say they can't get along anymore. They are getting a divorce.

Divorce is the **legal** ending of a **marriage**. Sometimes parents can't get along. Or the way they feel about each other changes.

Parents and children can't get divorced. They may not always get along. But they are always tied together. They may fight, but they always love each other.

It is important to know that divorce is not your fault. You didn't do anything wrong. You are not the reason your parents are divorcing.

CHAPTER 2

WHAT DOES IT MEAN?

Divorce changes families in different ways. But one thing stays the same. That is the fact that your parents want the best for you.

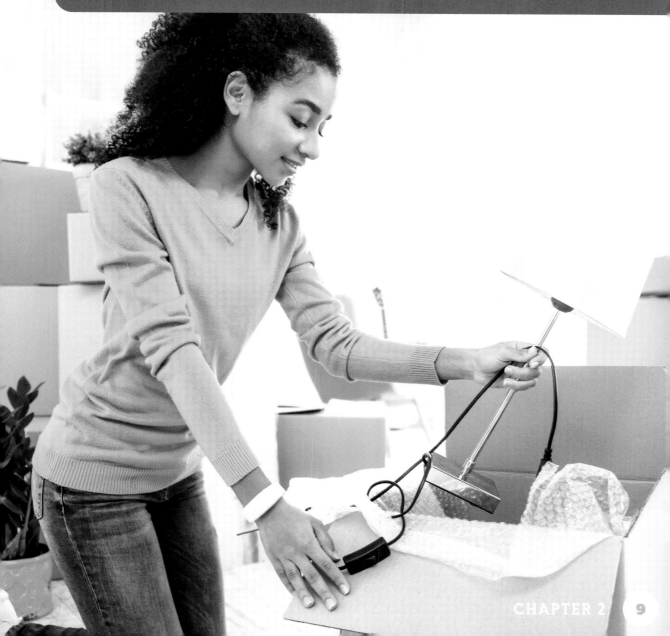

Divorce changes a family's daily life. Talk to your parents about what to expect. Lin's parents live apart after their divorce. She splits her time between both homes. She has two bedrooms.

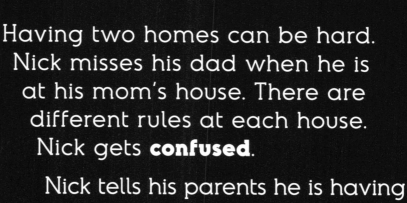

Having two homes can be hard. Nick misses his dad when he is at his mom's house. There are different rules at each house. Nick gets **confused**.

Nick tells his parents he is having a hard time. It is hard to talk about. But **communicating** is important. It helps him feel better. His parents help fix the problems.

PROCESS EMOTIONS

You may feel many **emotions** during a divorce. Journaling can help. Write down your thoughts. This can help you **identify** your feelings. It can help you **process** them.

You may not see one of your parents as much after a divorce. There may be a legal decision about when you can be with your parents. Jordan lives with his dad most of the time now. His mom doesn't love him any less. The time he spends with both is special.

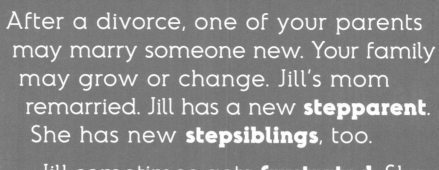

After a divorce, one of your parents may marry someone new. Your family may grow or change. Jill's mom remarried. Jill has a new **stepparent**. She has new **stepsiblings**, too.

Jill sometimes gets **frustrated**. She has to share her space and toys. At first, this is hard. But after she gets to know her stepsiblings, it's not so bad. They even play together!

SINGLE PARENTS

Not all parents remarry. Some become single parents. You might not see one of your parents at all after a divorce. Your family feels smaller, but it is still your family!

CHAPTER 3

WHAT ABOUT ME?

Everyone involved in the divorce will feel many emotions. The divorce isn't your choice. You don't get a say in what is happening. You may feel anger, sadness, **anxiety**, or **guilt**.

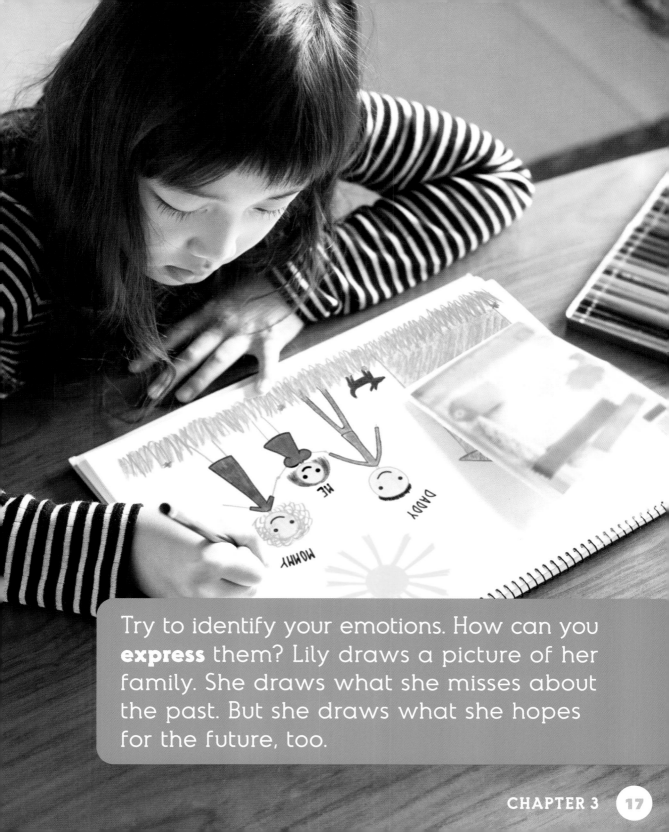

Try to identify your emotions. How can you **express** them? Lily draws a picture of her family. She draws what she misses about the past. But she draws what she hopes for the future, too.

Mason wants to talk to his parents. But it feels too hard. He doesn't want to hurt their feelings. And he knows they are having a hard time, too. What if he talks to them and it causes another fight?

Keeping his feelings inside isn't good for Mason. He needs to talk to someone. A **counselor** helps him talk about his feelings. She helps him talk to his parents, too.

Divorce is hard for everyone. It is important to identify your feelings and talk to your friends and family about them. Even if you feel sad, try to be positive. Your parents love you and want the best for you.

HELPING FRIENDS

Are your friend's parents divorcing? Your friend may act differently. Maybe he or she is quiet or doesn't want to play as much. This won't last forever. Let your friend know you are there to listen.

GOALS AND TOOLS

GROW WITH GOALS

Divorce is difficult to process. Here are a few things you can do after you learn of divorce in your family.

Goal: Think about what you are feeling. Name the emotions as they come. Talk about them with your parents.

Goal: It can feel like everything will change. Make a list of things that will stay the same after the divorce.

Goal: Start a journal. Draw or write how you are feeling each day. Talk to a sibling, parent, or friend about your feelings, too.

MINDFULNESS EXERCISE

Divorce can feel overwhelming. You may have many emotions at once. Mindfulness can help you be present and recognize your emotions.

- When you are feeling overwhelmed or need to take a moment, focus on your senses.

- Take a deep breath in. Slowly let it out.

- What do you see and hear?

- What do you smell and taste?

- What do you feel?

- Continue to focus on your senses for a few minutes. Focus on being in the moment.

GLOSSARY

anxiety
A feeling of worry or fear.

communicating
Sharing feelings, thoughts, or information.

confused
Uncertain or puzzled.

counselor
Someone trained to help with problems or give advice.

emotions
Feelings, such as happiness, sadness, or anger.

express
To show what you feel or think with words, writing, or actions.

frustrated
Angry and annoyed.

guilt
A feeling of shame for thinking you have done something wrong.

identify
To recognize what something is.

legal
Of or having to do with the law.

marriage
A legal relationship in which two people are joined as spouses.

process
To gain an understanding or acceptance of something.

stepparent
Someone a mother or father marries after a divorce.

stepsiblings
Brothers or sisters brought to a family by marriage after a divorce.

TO LEARN MORE

FACT SURFER

Finding more information is as easy as 1, 2, 3.

1. Go to www.factsurfer.com

2. Enter "**facingdivorce**" into the search box.

3. Choose your cover to see a list of websites.

INDEX

changes 5, 8, 9, 15

communicating 11

counselor 18

daily life 9

draws 17

emotions 11, 16, 17

express 17

fighting 4, 6, 18

friends 21

helps 11, 18, 21

homes 9, 11

hopes 17

journaling 11

legal decision 12

love 6, 12, 21

marriage 5

process 11

remarried 15

rules 11

share 15

single parents 15

stepparent 15

stepsiblings 15

talk 4, 9, 11, 18, 21

Blue Owl Books are published by Jump!, 5357 Penn Avenue South, Minneapolis, MN 55419, www.jumplibrary.com

Copyright © 2021 Jump! International copyright reserved in all countries. No part of this book may be reproduced in any form without written permission from the publisher.

Library of Congress Cataloging-in-Publication Data

Names: Finne, Stephanie, author.
Title: Facing divorce / by Stephanie Finne.
Description: Minneapolis: Jump!, Inc., [2021]
Series: Facing life's challenges | "Blue Owl Books." | Includes index. | Audience: Ages 7–10.
Identifiers: LCCN 2019057821 (print)
LCCN 2019057822 (ebook)
ISBN 9781645274131 (library binding)
ISBN 9781645274148 (paperback)
ISBN 9781645274155 (ebook)
Subjects: LCSH: Divorce—Juvenile literature. | Children of divorced parents—Juvenile literature.
Leadership—Juvenile literature.
Classification: LCC HQ814 .F5226 2021 (print) | LCC HQ814 (ebook) | DDC 306.89—dc23
LC record available at https://lccn.loc.gov/2019057821
LC ebook record available at https://lccn.loc.gov/2019057822

Editor: Jenna Gleisner
Designer: Jenna Casura

Photo Credits: Rawpixel.com/Shutterstock, cover (parents); michaeljung/Shutterstock, cover (child); Wavebreakmedia/iStock, 1 (parents); nuiiko/iStock, 1 (child); pathdoc/ Shutterstock, 3; diane39/iStock, 4; fizkes/Shutterstock, 5; imagesbybarbara/iStock, 6–7; kali9/iStock, 8; Zinkevych/iStock, 9; Monkey Business Images/Shutterstock, 10–11; omgimages/iStock, 12–13; Miaden Sladojevic/iStock, 14–15; AaronAmat/iStock, 16; Yagi-Studio/iStock, 17; Ievgenia Tiiechko/Shutterstock, 17 (drawing); New Africa/ Shutterstock, 18–19; digitalskillet/iStock, 20–21.

Printed in the United States of America at Corporate Graphics in North Mankato, Minnesota.